Italian Takeout Cookbook

Favorite Italian Takeout Recipes to Make at Home

Lina Chang

Copyrights

All rights reserved © Lina Chang and The Cookbook Publisher. No part of this publication or the information in it may be quoted from or reproduced in any form by means such as printing, scanning, photocopying, or otherwise without prior written permission of the copyright holder.

Disclaimer and Terms of Use

Effort has been made to ensure that the information in this book is accurate and complete. However, the author and the publisher do not warrant the accuracy of the information, text, and graphics contained within the book due to the rapidly changing nature of science, research, known and unknown facts, and internet. The author and the publisher do not hold any responsibility for errors, omissions, or contrary interpretation of the subject matter herein. This book is presented solely for motivational and informational purposes only.

The recipes provided in this book are for informational purposes only and are not intended to provide dietary advice. A medical practitioner should be consulted before making any changes in diet. Additionally, recipe cooking times may require adjustment depending on age and quality of appliances. Readers are strongly urged to take all precautions to ensure ingredients are fully cooked in order to avoid the dangers of foodborne illnesses. The recipes and suggestions provided in this book are solely the opinion of the author. The author and publisher do not take any responsibility for any consequences that may result due to following the instructions provided in this book.

ISBN: 978-1535576642

Printed in the United States

Contents

Introduction _____ 1
   History _____ 1
   Ingredients _____ 2
   Tools and Equipment _____ 5
   Cooking Methods _____ 6
Appetizers _____ 9
   Mozzarella Sticks _____ 9
   Deep-Fried Rice Balls (Arancini Di Riso) _____ 11
   Eggplant Parmesan (Parmigiana Di Melanzane) _____ 13
   Toast with Olive Oil, Garlic and Tomato (Bruschetta) _____ 15
   Appetizer Platter (Antipasto Misto Italiano) _____ 17
   Homemade Toasted Ravioli _____ 19
Soups _____ 21
   Minestrone _____ 21
   Pasta and Beans (Pasta e Fagioli) _____ 23
Rices _____ 25
   Creamy Mushrooms Risotto _____ 25
Salads _____ 27
   Caesar Salad _____ 27
   Capri's Tomato and Mozzarella Salad (Caprese Salad) _____ 30
   Italian Green Salad _____ 31
   Antipasto Salad _____ 33
   Pear Gorgonzola _____ 34
Sandwiches and Bread _____ 37
   Garlic Bread _____ 37
   Garlic Knots _____ 39
   Italian Sandwich _____ 41
   Grilled Vegetables Panini _____ 43
   Meatball Parmigiana Hero _____ 45
Pasta _____ 47
   Homemade and Handmade Pasta Dough _____ 47
   Gnocchi _____ 50
   Homemade Pasta Sauce (Marinara) _____ 53
   Spaghetti with Meat Sauce (Bolognese) _____ 55

- Spaghetti with Meatballs ___ 57
- Fettucine Alfredo ___ 59
- Classic Lasagna ___ 61
- Pasta with Vegetables (Primavera) ___ 64
- Creamy Pesto Linguini ___ 65
- Fettuccini Carbonara ___ 67
- Seafood Linguini (Linguini al Fruiti di Mare) ___ 69
- Shrimp in Spicy Sauce (Fra Diavolo) ___ 71
- Pasta with Capers, Olives and Tomato (Puttanesca) ___ 73

Pizza ___ 75
- Basic Pizza Dough ___ 75
- Homemade Pizza Sauce ___ 77
- Cheese Pizza ___ 79
- Hawaiian Pizza ___ 81
- Super Meat Pizza ___ 83
- Pepperoni Pizza ___ 85
- Pesto Veggie Pizza ___ 87
- Italian Spicy Sausage and Mushrooms Pizza ___ 89
- White Pizza (Pizza Bianca) with Chicken and Broccoli ___ 91
- BBQ Chicken Pizza ___ 93

Chicken ___ 95
- Chicken Marsala ___ 95
- Chicken Parmigiana ___ 97

Dessert (Dolci) ___ 101
- Tiramisu ___ 101
- Homemade Cannoli ___ 103

Conclusion ___ 107
Image Credits ___ 108
Also from Lina Chang ___ 109
Appendix ___ 110
Cooking Conversion Charts ___ 110

Introduction

Italian food is a part of American culture. Pizza and spaghetti are the icons of Italian-American cuisine. Though some may not accept Italian-American dishes as authentic, these dishes undoubtedly embody the things that best characterize Italian cuisine – passion, freshness, palatability and simplicity.

Food in Italy has always been regional, with each having its own distinct flavor or method of cooking. Perhaps America has become another "region" with its own distinct style of Italian cooking.

History

As with other immigrants, Italians, who came as early as 1880, brought their own dishes to the United States. The majority of the immigrants came from the southern parts of Italy such as Calabria, Abruzzi, and Sicily, and have left their mark on Italian-American cuisine.

These newcomers adjusted to the new environment by making use of available resources to create new dishes. Spaghetti with meatballs is one example. Where meat was reserved for special occasions back in Italy, the ready availability of ground beef gave way to the meatball. It was smothered with marinara sauce, which also became the most popular sauce because canned tomatoes were readily available. The same thing happened with spaghetti – one of the few other Italian ingredients then available in the US.

Aside from the immigrants, soldiers coming after World War II began looking for the Italian cuisine which they had sampled while stationed in Italy. This gave rise to more establishments rising to meet this new market.

From the modest pizza from Naples, which usually consisted of basil, garlic, and tomato; American pizza, with tomato sauce and a variety of toppings, has evolved.
American cities now have their own signature "Italian" dishes such as the Philly cheese steak of Philadelphia, the muffuletta sandwich of New Orleans, and chicken tetrazzini, as well as cioppino of San Francisco.

Today, America is willingly embracing authentic dishes as diverse ingredients are now easy to find. Many new restaurants have opened up, selling real Italian food as well as fusion dishes, blending Italian and other American flavors and ingredients.

Ingredients

Olive oil, garlic, and herbs are said to be the basic ingredients in Italian cooking. These, together with the ingredients listed here, will help you begin you Italian cooking journey.

Balsamic Vinegar (*Aceto Balsamico*)
A sweet-sour vinegar from Italy made from reduced and aged juice of Trebbiano grapes. It is used for marinades, dips, sauces, and salad dressing.

Basil (*Basilico*)
Preferably fresh. Basil has become known as the herb that is distinctively Italian. Sweet basil is commonly used for sauces, salads, and soups.

Beans (*Fagioli*)
These are common in soup, pasta, and stews. Popular beans are cannellini (white kidney beans), fava beans, and chickpeas.

Cheeses (*Formaggio*)
Italian cheeses are very diverse as almost every region in Italy has its own variety. Cheese is used for pasta, sandwiches, pizza, and desserts. Well-known cheeses are Asiago, fontina, Gorgonzola, mascarpone, mozzarella, and Parmigiano-Reggiano (Parmesan cheese).

Garlic (*Aglio*)
Italians use a lot of garlic for soups, stews, sauces and for grilled meat.

Herbs (*Odori*)
Oregano, sage, and thyme are often used to add flavor to dishes.

Mortar and Pestle
For crushing vegetables and herbs.

Pasta
Thin sauces are said to go best with thin pasta, while tubular pasta goes well with thicker sauces. More well-known pastas are spaghetti, lasagna, macaroni, fettuccine, rotini, linguine, penne, cannelloni, and rigatoni.

Olive Oil (*Olio d'Oliva*)
This is a staple of Italian dishes. Oils from different regions have slightly different flavors. Extra-virgin, first- and cold-pressed are said to be high quality. DOP or 'denomination of origin' denotes that it meets the standards of the local government. Extra-virgin is recommended by chefs to be used for dressings and finishing while regular olive oil may be used for longer or high-temperature cooking.

Rice
Arborio or *Carnaroli* are preferred as they have a creamy consistency when cooked, which is desirable in *risotto*.

Tomato (*Pomodoro*)
Italian-American dishes make more use of canned tomato, tomato sauce, and tomato paste, as these were what Italian immigrants found to be more conveniently available in the past, where the same dishes in Italy would have called for fresh tomato. This may be one of the main differences between Americanized Italian dishes and authentic dishes.

Wine (*Vino*)
Red and white wines are used to enhance the flavor of dishes. Marsala is a sweet wine used for dishes like Chicken Marsala. It may be substituted with brandy, sherry, or port.

Tools and Equipment

A conventionally well-equipped kitchen is all you need to prepare Italian dishes. To make homemade pasta and pizza dough, some extra equipment may be needed.

Cheese Grater
Choose one with at least 2 sides and grating sizes. Soft cheese like mozzarella requires a larger grating size, while harder cheese like Parmesan would require a smaller grating size. A rotary grater is also useful, especially for grating large amounts of cheese.

Garlic Press
This is very handy as Italian cooking requires handling a lot of garlic. The garlic clove can be inserted unpeeled into the press for crushing.

Knives
Various sizes will come in handy for cutting meat and vegetables.

Pasta Maker
Recommended, if one intends to make homemade pasta. With this and a good pasta dough, any cook can easily make a variety of pastas using different attachments.

Pasta Drying Rack
A rack with "arms" for hanging freshly-formed pasta and to help them keep the right shape while drying.

Pizza Cutter or Pizza Wheel
For convenient cutting of cooked pizza, pastry, or uncooked dough.

Pizza Peel
A shovel-like tool used for safely and easily putting in or removing the pizza from a hot oven. It is usually made of wood, although it may also be metal.

Pizza Stone
A kind of cooking surface for pizza dough, made of stone, ceramic, firebrick, or other materials. Although any baking sheet or tray will do, the pizza stone is said to yield a better-tasting and better-textured pizza crust.

Pot with Draining Basket
For convenient cooking of pasta. After cooking, one can pull out the pasta to drain it quickly.

Wooden Spoons
Keep many different sizes on hand for mixing sauces, batters, and various other mixtures.

Cooking Methods

Italian cooking is usually quick and simple, with more focus given to the quality and freshness of the ingredients. Common cooking methods such as boiling, steaming, sautéing, braising, frying, stewing and grilling are used.

The braising of meat is done by cooking slowly in a tight-lidded pot with vinegar, wine, water, broth, or tomatoes. This is done to tenderize the meat and build flavor.

In sautéing, ingredients are cooked in hot oil, and flavors are enhanced by reduction and caramelization. Grapeseed or other cooking oils, not olive oil, are used for deep-frying.

Pasta is made tastier by allowing it to absorb flavor from the sauce. This is done by removing the pasta a minute before it is expected to be done, and cooking it in the sauce with a little of its cooking water for a minute or two. Italians prefer pasta *al dente,* or firm to the bite, so they may cook pasta for a shorter time than indicated in the packaging.

Now that you have your kitchen equipped with the basic ingredients and equipment, it's time to try cooking some truly delicious Italian takeout dishes!

Appetizers

Mozzarella Sticks

Serves: 12
Preparation Time: 10 minutes
Cooking Time: 5 minutes

Ingredients
1 cup Italian style bread crumbs
2 eggs
1 tablespoon milk
1 pound mozzarella cheese, cut into ¾-inch x ¾-inch strips
1 cup vegetable oil
Tomato sauce for dipping
Fresh basil for garnish

Directions
1. In a bowl, whisk the eggs and milk together.
2. Place the bread crumbs in another bowl, or on a tray.
3. Dip the cheese in the egg mixture first, then the bread crumbs.
4. Dip it in the egg mixture and then the bread crumbs a second time, making sure to coat the cheese evenly.
5. Heat the oil in skillet.
6. Fry the cheese until golden brown, about 1 minute on each side. Do not fry too long, or the cheese will leak.
7. Drain on paper towels.
8. Serve with tomato sauce and sprinkle with finely chopped basil.

Deep-Fried Rice Balls (Arancini Di Riso)

Serves: 4-6
Preparation Time: 15 minutes
Cooking Time: 15 minutes

Ingredients
1 cup Italian style seasoned bread crumbs

For filling
2 cups cooked risotto, cooled
½ cup Italian style seasoned bread crumbs
½ cup Parmesan, finely grated
¼ cup fresh basil leaves, finely chopped
2 eggs, beaten
4 ounces Gorgonzola, cut into ½-inch cubes
Vegetable oil, for frying

Directions
1. Put the bread crumbs in a medium bowl, and set them aside.
2. Combine the risotto, bread crumbs, Parmesan, basil, and eggs.
3. Scoop out about 2 tablespoons of the risotto mixture at a time, and shape it into 1 ¾-inch balls. Dampen your hands so the rice doesn't stick them.
4. Insert a cube of Gorgonzola into each ball, and seal to cover the cheese.
5. Coat the balls with bread crumbs.
6. Fill a heavy-bottomed skillet or saucepan with oil to about 2-3 inches deep.
7. Heat over medium heat until a cube of bread will brown in about 2 minutes (350°F).
8. Fry the balls, turning occasionally, until golden, about 4 to 5 minutes. Do not overcrowd the pan.
9. Drain on paper towels and serve.

Eggplant Parmesan (Parmigiana Di Melanzane)

Serves: 6
Preparation Time: 20 minutes
Cooking Time: 45 minutes

Ingredients
2 eggplants, peeled and cut into ½-inch slices

For eggplant slices
1 tablespoon salt, or as needed, preferably kosher or sea salt
1 cup Italian style bread crumbs
¼ cup grated Parmesan cheese
2 eggs, beaten

For eggplant parmigiana layers
1 (28 ounce) jar garlic-and-tomato pasta sauce or homemade pasta sauce

¼ cup grated Parmesan cheese
4 cups or 16 ounces mozzarella cheese, shredded
½ teaspoon dried basil

Directions
1. Sprinkle both sides of each slice of eggplant generously with salt. Place the eggplant slices in a colander and allow them to "sweat" for 1-3 hours.
2. After the standing time, wipe the eggplant slices dry with paper towels.
3. When the eggplant slices are ready, preheat the oven to 350°F and grease a baking sheet.
4. In a bowl, mix the bread crumbs with Parmesan.
5. Dip the eggplant into the beaten eggs and then coat with the breadcrumb mixture.
6. Place the pieces on the baking sheet in a single layer.
7. Bake until lightly browned on both sides (about 6-10 minutes per side)
8. Now prepare to layer the sauce, eggplant, and cheeses.
9. In a 9x13 baking pan, start with a layer of pasta sauce.
10. Follow this with a layer of eggplant.
11. Sprinkle the eggplant with about 1 tablespoon of Parmesan and 1 to 1 ⅓ cups shredded mozzarella.
12. Continue layering, making sure to end with a cheese layer.
13. Sprinkle with basil and bake until the cheese turns golden brown (about 35 minutes).

Toast with Olive Oil, Garlic and Tomato (Bruschetta)

Serves: 4-6
Preparation Time: 10 minutes
Cooking Time: 15 minutes

Ingredients
1 baguette, cut in half lengthwise and toasted slightly
¼ cup grated Parmesan cheese
½ cup mozzarella, shredded (optional)

For topping
2 teaspoons minced garlic (fresh or from a jar)
3 tablespoons extra-virgin olive oil
2 ½ cups minced tomatoes, finely chopped
⅓ cup fresh basil leaf, thinly sliced
2 tablespoons balsamic vinegar
½ teaspoon salt
1 teaspoon freshly ground pepper

Directions
1. Combine the topping ingredients and let them sit for 15 minutes, to allow flavors to develop.
2. Slice the toasted baguette into sections for serving.
3. Top with tomato mixture and sprinkle with the cheeses, if desired
4. Toast to melt the cheese (about 5-10 minutes).

Appetizer Platter (Antipasto Misto Italiano)

Serves: 6
Preparation Time: 15 minutes
Cooking Time: 0 minutes

Ingredients
3 cups mozzarella cheese (or cheese of choice like provolone or bocconcini), torn, sliced or cubed
20 slices prosciutto (or other Italian cold cuts like pancetta, pepperoni, salami, capicola, etc.)
3 (8 ½ or 10 ounce) jars of vegetables in olive oil (olive, artichoke, tomato, giardiniera, mushroom, peppers, onions, etc.), drained, oil reserved
3 tablespoons mixed olives
½ cup cherry tomatoes, halved
Parmesan, for shaving
1 loaf ciabatta bread, sliced and toasted
1 clove garlic, crushed into a paste

<u>For basil-flavored oil</u>
1 cup fresh basil, stems removed
⅛ teaspoon salt
3 tablespoons reserved oil from the vegetables

Directions
1. Arrange the ingredients in small piles on a large plate. The aim is to get a "rustic" look.
2. Sprinkle the cold cuts with some shaved Parmesan.
3. Use a mortar and pestle to crush the basil and salt into a paste. Mix this with some of the reserved oil.
4. Drizzle the basil-flavored oil over the cheese and vegetables. Drizzle more olive oil over the platter, if desired.
5. Rub the garlic on the ciabatta toast and drizzle lightly with olive oil. Add this to the platter and serve. If the meats are cold, allow them to come to room temperature before serving.

Homemade Toasted Ravioli

Serves: 6-8
Preparation Time: 30 minutes
Cooking Time: 20 minutes

Ingredients
1 (16 ounce) package beef ravioli, fresh or thawed
2 cups flour
2 large eggs, beaten
¼ cup water
2 cups Italian bread crumbs
1 teaspoon garlic salt
Vegetable oil, for deep frying
Marinara sauce for dipping

Directions
1. Preheat a deep fryer to 350°F.
2. In a bowl, whisk the eggs and water together.
3. In another bowl, combine the bread crumbs and garlic salt.

4. Dip the thawed ravioli in flour, then the egg mixture, and then coat them thickly with bread crumbs. Dip in the egg again, if needed, to coat evenly.
5. Place the coated ravioli on a sheet of aluminum or tray.
6. Fry the ravioli, a few at a time, until golden brown (about 1 minute).
7. Drain on paper towels, and serve with marinara sauce.

Soups

Minestrone

Serves: 8
Preparation Time: 0 minutes
Cooking Time: 45 minutes

Ingredients
3 tablespoons olive oil
1 small onion, minced
½ stalk celery, minced
4 cloves garlic, minced
1 cup frozen Italian cut green beans
½ cup zucchini, diced
4 cups vegetable broth

1 (14 ounce) can diced tomatoes
2 (15 ounce) cans red kidney beans, drained
1 (15 ounce) can small white beans or great northern beans, drained
½ cup carrot, julienned
3 cups hot water
2 tablespoons fresh parsley, minced
1 ½ teaspoons dried oregano
1 ½ teaspoons salt
½ teaspoon ground black pepper, or to taste
½ teaspoon dried basil
¼ teaspoon dried thyme
4 cups fresh baby spinach or sliced cabbage
½ cup small shell pasta
½ cup red wine

Directions
1. Heat the olive oil over medium heat in a large pot.
2. Sauté the onion, celery, garlic, green beans, and zucchini until the onions begin to turn translucent (about 5 minutes).
3. Add the vegetable broth, drained tomatoes, beans, carrot, hot water, and spices (parsley through thyme).
4. Bring the soup to a boil, then reduce the heat and simmer for 20 minutes.
5. Add the spinach leaves or cabbage, pasta, and red wine.
6. Cook until the pasta has the desired consistency (about 20 minutes).

Pasta and Beans (Pasta e Fagioli)

Serves: 6-8
Preparation Time: 5 minutes
Cooking Time: 30 minutes

Ingredients
1 tablespoon olive oil
1 pound ground beef
¼ cup diced pancetta (optional)
1 small onion, diced
2 small carrots, sliced
1 small red bell pepper, diced
1 (28 ounce) can diced tomatoes, undrained
1 (16 ounce) can white kidney beans, drained
2 cups beef stock
1 ½ teaspoons oregano
1 teaspoon pepper
3 teaspoons parsley
1 (10 ounce) jar tomato sauce

1 cup ditalini or pasta of choice, cooked according to packaging instructions
Grated Parmesan

Directions
1. Heat the oil and brown the beef in a skillet.
2. Add the pancetta (optional) and sauté until lightly browned.
3. Add the onion, carrots, and pepper and sauté until tender (about 5 minutes).
4. Transfer the mixture to a soup pot, draining away the fat.
5. Add the rest of the ingredients EXCEPT the pasta and Parmesan, and bring them to a boil. Reduce the heat to simmer.
6. Simmer, stirring occasionally, until the vegetables are tender and the soup has the desired thickness (8-10 minutes).
7. Add the cooked ditalini, and cook to heat through (about 1 minute).
8. Serve sprinkled with grated Parmesan.

Rices

Creamy Mushrooms Risotto

Serves: 2
Preparation Time: 5 minutes
Cooking Time: 30-35 minutes

Ingredients
2 cups chicken broth
3 tablespoons unsalted butter, softened
½ small onion, chopped
½ cup Portobello mushrooms, sliced
¾ cup Arborio rice
¼ cup dry white wine
¼ cup Parmesan, finely grated
Salt and freshly-ground pepper, to taste

Directions
1. Pour the broth into a medium saucepan, and bring it to a simmer.
2. Reduce the heat to low, to keep the broth hot.
3. Melt 2 tablespoons of the butter over medium heat.
4. Sauté the onion and mushrooms until tender (about 3 minutes). Remove mushrooms and set them aside.
5. Add the rice and mix well.
6. Add the wine and simmer until almost dry (about 1 minute).
7. Add half a cup of hot broth and cook, with stirring, until it is absorbed by the rice (about 2 minutes). Repeat, half a cup at a time.
8. Allow complete absorption before adding more broth. The rice should be creamy in consistency, but the grains should be tender yet firm to the bite (about 20 minutes).
9. Turn off the heat and stir in the remaining butter, Parmesan cheese, salt, pepper and mushrooms.

Salads

Caesar Salad

Serves: 6
Preparation Time: 10 minutes
Cooking Time: 10 minutes

Ingredients
Caesar Salad Dressing
2 small cloves garlic, minced
1 teaspoon anchovy paste
Juice of 1 lemon
1 teaspoon Dijon mustard
1 teaspoon Worcestershire sauce
1 cup mayonnaise
½ cup freshly grated Parmigiano-Reggiano
¼ teaspoon salt
¼ teaspoon freshly ground black pepper

Croutons
2 tablespoons butter
2 tablespoons extra virgin olive oil
2 cloves garlic, halved
3 cups French or Italian bread, sliced into ½-inch cubes
Salt and pepper

For salad
½ cup Parmesan cheese, shredded, plus more for topping if desired
2 heads romaine lettuce, torn into bite-sized pieces

Directions

For the dressing
1. Whisk together the garlic, anchovy paste, lemon juice, Dijon mustard, and Worcestershire sauce.
2. Add the mayonnaise, Parmigiano-Reggiano, salt, and pepper. Mix well.
3. Taste and adjust the proportions to your liking.
4. Will keep, refrigerated, for 2 weeks.

For the croutons
5. Preheat the oven to 350°F.
6. Heat the butter, olive oil, and garlic in a saucepan over low heat.
7. Remove the saucepan from the heat as soon as the butter has melted.
8. Let it stand for 10 minutes, and then remove the garlic.
9. Toss in the bread cubes, and mix to coat.
10. Spread the bread cubes on the baking sheet, and bake until the croutons are golden brown (about 10 minutes), shaking the pan once or twice.
11. Remove the pan from the oven and set it aside to cool.

To assemble the salad
12. Toss the lettuce and croutons in the dressing until well coated.
13. Sprinkle on the Parmesan cheese and toss lightly.
14. Sprinkle more Parmesan on top, if desired, and serve.

Capri's Tomato and Mozzarella Salad (Caprese Salad)

Serves: 4-6
Preparation Time: 45 minutes
Cooking Time: 0 minutes

Ingredients
4 large tomatoes, sliced ¼ inch thick
1 pound fresh mozzarella, sliced ¼ inch thick
¼ cup packed fresh basil, washed and dried
⅓ teaspoon dried oregano, crumbled
3 tablespoons extra-virgin olive oil
Fine sea salt, to taste
Freshly ground black pepper, to taste

Directions
1. Layer the tomato and mozzarella slices alternately on a serving dish.
2. Sprinkle with oregano and drizzle with olive oil.
3. Season with salt and pepper.

Italian Green Salad

Serves: 4
Preparation Time: 2 hours refrigeration
Cooking Time: 0 minutes

Ingredients
For dressing
¼ cup white vinegar
2 tablespoons sugar
½ cup mayonnaise
2 cloves garlic
½ teaspoon Italian seasoning
½ teaspoon dried parsley
1 teaspoon olive oil
Juice of half a lemon
¼ cup Parmesan cheese

For the salad
1 head lettuce, chopped
2 tomatoes, cut into wedges
½ can medium black olives
2 cups croutons
8 pepperoncini peppers
2 cups mozzarella cheese, shaved or torn into small pieces
½ teaspoon salt
1 teaspoon pepper

Directions
For the dressing
1. Place all the ingredients in a blender, and blend until smooth.
2. Refrigerate for at least 2 hours.

To assemble the salad
   3. Combine the ingredients and toss well.
   4. Serve with the dressing on the side, or add the dressing to the salad and toss well.

Antipasto Salad

Serves: 4
Preparation Time: 10 minutes
Cooking Time: 0 minutes

Ingredients
8 cups romaine lettuce heart, chopped
¼ pound Genoa salami, diced
¼ pound pepperoni, diced
2 cups giardiniera (Italian pickled vegetables), coarsely chopped
12 pitted black olives, coarsely chopped
12 jumbo green olives, pitted, coarsely chopped
1 (8 ounce) jar roasted red peppers, drained and diced
1 (6 ounce) jar marinated artichoke hearts, drained
¼ red onion, sliced into rings
2 tablespoons balsamic vinegar
¼ cup extra-virgin olive oil
1-2 tablespoons Italian Vinaigrette (optional)
Salt, to taste
Freshly ground pepper, to taste
½ cup Gorgonzola, crumbled (optional)

Directions
1. Combine first 9 ingredients (through red onion) in a bowl.
2. Season with salt and pepper, and then drizzle with olive oil and balsamic vinegar and/or Italian Vinaigrette (optional).
3. Toss well. Garnish with crumbled cheese, if desired.

Pear Gorgonzola

Serves: 2
Preparation Time: 15 minutes plus 30 minutes sitting time
Cooking Time: 1 hour

Ingredients
Italian Vinaigrette
⅓ cup white wine vinegar

¾ teaspoon dried oregano
½ teaspoon dry mustard
1 teaspoon salt
1 pinch black pepper
⅛ cup red onion, finely chopped
1 ½ teaspoons garlic, minced
¾ cup olive oil

Spiced Walnuts
1 egg white
1 tablespoon water
2 cups walnuts, halves and pieces
½ cup sugar
1 teaspoon cinnamon
½ teaspoon allspice

For the salad
1 red pear, cored and thinly sliced
3 cups mixed greens, washed and chopped
2 tablespoons Gorgonzola cheese, crumbled, plus more for garnish
½ cup spiced walnuts, chopped
¼ cup dried cranberries
½ cup Italian vinaigrette

Directions
For the spiced walnuts
1. Preheat the oven to 225°F, and line a shallow baking pan with foil.
2. In a bowl, whisk the egg white and water together until frothy.
3. Toss in the walnuts and mix to coat.
4. Using a strainer, let them drain for 3 minutes.
5. In a plastic bag, shake together the sugar, cinnamon, and allspice.

6. Add the walnuts, seal the bag, and shake to coat walnuts.
7. Spread the nuts in a single layer on the foil-lined baking sheet.
8. Bake for 1 hour, stirring every 15 minutes.
9. Cool completely and store in an air-tight jar.

For the vinaigrette
10. Put all the ingredients, EXCEPT the olive oil, in a blender.
11. Pulse a few times and then blend, adding the olive oil a little at a time. Do not add the olive oil all at once.
12. Blend well and let it stand for 30 minutes.

For the salad
13. While the nuts are baking and the vinaigrette is sitting, prepare the pear and lettuce.
14. Once everything is ready, mix the vinaigrette into the lettuce.
15. Add the other ingredients and toss well.
16. Garnish with more crumbled cheese and serve.

Sandwiches and Bread

Garlic Bread

Serves: 4-6
Preparation Time: 10 minutes
Cooking Time: 30 minutes

Ingredients
2 teaspoons garlic, finely chopped
¼ teaspoon salt
¼ cup unsalted butter, softened
1 tablespoon extra-virgin olive oil
2 tablespoons fresh flat-leaf parsley, finely chopped
1 loaf Italian bread, about 15 inches long, 3-4 inches wide

Directions

1. Preheat the oven to 350°F.
2. Using a mortar and pestle, mash the garlic with the salt until it forms a paste. Transfer it to a bowl.
3. Add the butter and oil. Mix until smooth.
4. Stir in the parsley.
5. Without cutting completely through the bottom, cut the bread to make slices about 1 inch thick.
6. Spread garlic butter between the slices.
7. Wrap the loaf in foil. At this point bread may be kept chilled and then thawed to room temperature.
8. Bake for 15 minutes.
9. Open foil and bake 5 minutes more. Separate the slices as you serve.

Garlic Knots

Serves: 24
Preparation Time: 45 minutes plus 2 hours proofing time
Cooking Time: 20 minutes

Ingredients
1 recipe Basic Pizza Dough
½ cup unsalted butter
3 tablespoons garlic, minced
1 tablespoon olive oil
1 teaspoon coarse sea salt
¼ cup grated Pecorino Romano or Parmesan cheese
2 tablespoons chopped fresh parsley

Directions
1. Prepare a batch of Basic Pizza Dough and set it aside to rise.
2. Cook the garlic in the butter in a small saucepan over low heat until fragrant (about 3 minutes).
3. Cover, remove the saucepan from the heat, and set it aside, keeping it warm.
4. Preheat the oven to 375°F, and grease 2 large baking sheets. Set them aside.
5. Place the risen dough on a lightly floured surface.
6. Roll the dough out using a floured rolling pin. Shape it into a rectangle, about 16x12 inches.
7. Brush the dough with olive oil.
8. Cut the dough in half lengthwise.
9. Cut the dough crosswise into 1 ¼-inch strips.
10. Tie each strip loosely into a knot, and place them on the prepared baking sheets, leaving a 2-inch space in between. Sprinkle the tops of the knots with salt.
11. Cover with a towel and let them rise in a warm place for about 30 minutes.
12. Bake until golden brown, about 20 minutes.
13. Meanwhile, add the cheese and parsley to the warm butter mixture and mix well.
14. Coat the newly baked knots in the cheese-and-butter mixture, and serve warm.

Italian Sandwich

Serves: 2
Preparation Time: 10 minutes
Cooking Time: 0 minutes

Ingredients
2 12-inch Italian style hoagie or sub rolls
¼ pound thinly sliced prosciutto or mortadella
¼ pound thinly sliced capicola
¼ pound thinly sliced provolone cheese
¼ pound thinly sliced Genoa salami
4-6 large lettuce leaves
1 thinly sliced large tomato
1 thinly sliced white onion
2 tablespoons olive oil, divided
4 teaspoons red wine vinegar, divided
Salt, pepper, Italian oregano
Pepperonata or fried sweet peppers (optional)

Directions
1. Slice each roll horizontally, but not all the way through.
2. For each one, layer on about 4 slices each of prosciutto, capicola, provolone cheese, and Genoa salami.
3. Top with lettuce, tomato, onion, 1 tablespoon of oil, 2 teaspoons of vinegar, salt, pepper, oregano and pepperonata (optional).
4. Slice and serve.

Grilled Vegetables Panini

Serves: 4
Preparation Time: 15 minutes
Cooking Time: 10 minutes

Ingredients
1 medium eggplant, sliced diagonally into ¼-inch strips
1 medium onion, peeled and sliced into ¼-inch rounds
1 red bell pepper, stem and seeds removed, sliced into 8 pieces
1 medium yellow squash or zucchini, sliced into ¼-inch strips
½ cup canola oil, divided
Salt and black pepper
1 tablespoon garlic, minced

1 tablespoon Italian seasoning
¼ cup red wine vinegar
Salt and freshly ground black pepper
¼ cup green olives, finely chopped
½ cup shredded mozzarella
4 panini sandwich buns

Directions
1. Preheat the grill to medium heat.
2. Brush the vegetables with about ¼ cup of the canola oil, season them with salt and pepper, and grill them until they are soft and slightly charred (about 3 minutes per side). Transfer them to a tray or baking sheet.
3. To make the dressing, whisk together the garlic, Italian seasoning, vinegar, the remaining ¼ cup of canola oil, and salt and pepper to taste.
4. Drizzle half of the dressing over the grilled vegetables.
5. Stir the chopped olives into the remaining dressing.
6. Spread the olive dressing on the bottom of the each panini and then layer the vegetables on the bread.
7. Sprinkle with cheese and cover with the top pieces of bread.
8. Grill the sandwiches or toast them in a Panini press (about 5 minutes).

Meatball Parmigiana Hero

Serves: 4
Preparation Time: 5 minutes
Cooking Time: 23 minutes

Ingredients

2 cups Traditional Italian Sauce (store bought or homemade)
16 1-ounce meatballs, fully-cooked, frozen
4 long submarine or hoagies rolls, split
1 cup shredded mozzarella cheese
Grated Parmesan cheese

Directions

1. Heat the meatballs in the sauce by bringing it to a boil and then simmering for 3 minutes.
2. Adjust the heat to low and cook for 20 minutes, stirring occasionally.
3. Spoon the meatballs and sauce into the rolls.
4. Sprinkle with the mozzarella and Parmesan.

Pasta

Homemade and Handmade Pasta Dough

Serves: 6
Preparation Time: 45 minutes plus 1 hour resting time for dough
Cooking Time: 3 minutes

Ingredients

1 pound (3 ⅓ cups) all-purpose flour
4 whole eggs plus 1 yolk
¼ cup extra-virgin olive oil
⅛ teaspoon kosher salt
1 to 2 tablespoons water, or as if needed

Directions

1. Pile the flour on a clean dry work surface, in a heap about 8 inches wide.
2. Make a well in the center.
3. Crack all the eggs and the pour the extra yolk into the well and add the olive oil, salt, and water.
4. Using a fork, beat the eggs together with the olive oil, water and salt. Be careful not to break the sides of the well or the egg mixture will run. You may do this in a bowl, if you fear that the liquid will run all over the work surface.
5. Using the fork, begin to incorporate the flour into the egg mixture. The dough may be lumpy.
6. When liquid ingredients are well incorporated and the mixture is no longer runny, start mixing it with your hands. You can wet your hands first if the dough is dry.
7. When the mixture has become homogeneous, begin kneading on floured surface. Again, wet your hands if the dough seems too dry and stiff.
8. Use your body weight to stretch and not tear the dough. Use the heels of your palms and knead until it is smooth and velvety (about 8-15 minutes).
9. Wrap the dough in plastic and let it rest for at least 1 hour. It may be refrigerated or frozen for later use.

10. To shape, the dough should be at room temperature.
11. Roll and cut it into the desired shape.
12. To cook, boil in about 6 quarts of water for 1 pound of pasta.
13. Freshly-made pasta will cook in 1-3 minutes.

Gnocchi

Serves: 12
Preparation Time: 35 minutes
Cooking Time: 45 minutes boiling potatoes plus 2-5 minutes cooking gnocchi

Ingredients
3 pounds russet or Idaho potatoes
2 cups all-purpose flour
1 egg, extra large
1 pinch salt
½ cup canola oil, if needed
Pasta sauce, homemade or store-bought
Grated Parmesan

Directions

1. Boil the potatoes, unpeeled, until they are soft (about 45 minutes).
2. Peel the potatoes while they are still warm (they will become soggy as they cool down) and pass them through a vegetable mill or ricer onto a clean pasta board. (Alternatively, you can use a grater.)
3. Let them cool to room temperature.
4. Make a well in the center of the potatoes, and sprinkle all the flour over.
5. Place the egg and salt in the center of the well and, using a fork, stir until the egg is well incorporated.
6. Dust your hands with flour and bring dough together.
7. Knead gently until the dough is smooth and soft but not elastic (about 4 minutes). To test, drop a pinch in boiling water. The dough is ready if it doesn't dissolve in the water.
8. Form a ball with the dough and flatten it slightly. Cut it into 8 equal wedges.
9. Take a wedge and roll out a ½-inch diameter rope.
10. Cut the rope into ½-inch pieces. Do the same with the other wedges.
11. At this point, begin preparing the water for cooking the gnocchi. Boil 6 quarts of water in a large pot. Prepare 6 cups of ice water to cool cooked gnocchi rapidly, if you intend to store it for later.
12. Meanwhile, to shape the gnocchi, take a fork and roll a piece of the cut dough down the back side of the tines. Place them on a floured tray and

cover with a towel. These may be covered with plastic wrap and frozen for later use.
13. To cook, drop these pieces (if frozen, do not thaw) into boiling water and cook, with gentle stirring, until they float (about 1 minute). Cook in batches, and do not crowd.
14. Use a slotted spoon or spider strainer to remove the gnocchi and transfer it to a serving dish.
15. At this point, you may cool the cooked the gnocchi in ice water, drain and toss with ½ cup of canola oil. Store it, covered, in the refrigerator for up to 48 hours.
16. To serve fresh, cooked gnocchi, top it with warm sauce and sprinkle with grated Parmesan.

Homemade Pasta Sauce (Marinara)

Serves: 4-6
Preparation Time: 20 minutes
Cooking Time: 35 minutes to 2 hours

Ingredients
8 large fresh tomatoes or 12 Roma tomatoes, seeded and diced into small pieces, OR 2 cans diced tomatoes
½ cup olive oil
8 cloves fresh garlic, minced
¾ cup fresh basil, minced OR 1 tablespoon dried basil
½ teaspoon salt
1 teaspoon fresh ground black pepper

Optional ingredients
¼ teaspoon red pepper flakes, crushed
1 teaspoon sugar
⅛ teaspoon each marjoram and/or oregano
Parmesan cheese

Directions
1. In a large skillet or saucepan, heat the olive oil over medium heat.
2. Sauté the garlic and cook until it is tender.
3. Add the tomatoes and cook until they are heated through.
4. Stir in the basil and the rest of the ingredients EXCEPT the Parmesan. Simmer until the sauce has the desired thickness (35 minutes for "fresher" sauce or 2 hours for thicker consistency).
5. Serve the sauce over cooked pasta, and sprinkle with Parmesan cheese.

Spaghetti with Meat Sauce (Bolognese)

Serves: 10
Preparation Time: 5 minutes
Cooking Time: 35 minutes

Ingredients
2 (24 ounce) jars Marinara sauce or 3 cups homemade pasta sauce
1 (16 ounce) can crushed tomatoes
1 onion, chopped
2 tablespoons olive oil
1 pound ground beef
1 pound Italian sausage, casings removed
½ cup pepperoni, finely chopped
1 teaspoon Italian seasonings or a combination of basil, oregano, rosemary, and thyme to taste
¼ cup red wine (preferably Chianti or Sangiovese)

10 ounces spaghetti noodles, cooked according to the packaging instructions

Directions
1. In a large pot, heat the olive oil and onions over medium-high heat. Cook until the onions are translucent.
2. Add the marina sauce and crushed tomatoes, and reduce the heat to simmer.
3. Meanwhile, in a skillet, brown the ground beef and Italian sausage until well done.
4. Drain out any excess fat, and add the meat to the pot with the sauce.
5. Add the chopped pepperoni, Italian seasonings, and red wine.
6. Simmer for about 20 minutes and season with salt and pepper.
7. Pour the sauce over cooked spaghetti noodles. Sprinkle with grated Parmesan, if desired.

Spaghetti with Meatballs

Serves: 6-8
Preparation Time: 15 minutes
Cooking Time: 45 minutes

Ingredients
2 (30 ounce) jars of spaghetti sauce or 3 ¾ cups homemade pasta sauce
1 pound spaghetti, cooked al dente

For meatballs
2 pounds lean ground beef
2 eggs
¾ cup dry bread crumbs
¼ cup fresh parsley, chopped
2 garlic cloves, minced
½ teaspoon salt or to taste
¼ cup Parmesan cheese

Directions

1. Combine the meatball ingredients in a bowl, mixing thoroughly.
2. Shape the mixture into 18 meatballs.
3. In a saucepan, bring the sauce to a simmer.
4. Add meatballs and return to a simmer.
5. Cover and cook until the meatballs are cooked through (about 35-40 minutes).
6. Serve the sauce and meatballs over warm spaghetti.

Fettucine Alfredo

Serves: 2-3
Preparation Time: 5 minutes
Cooking Time: 15 minutes

Ingredients
1 (8 ounce) package fettucine, cooked according to packaging instructions and drained
¼ cup water, reserved from cooking pasta
3 tablespoons unsalted butter
1 small shallot, finely minced
½ cup heavy cream
¾ cup freshly Parmigiano-Reggiano or Parmesan, grated
¼ teaspoon salt
Freshly ground black pepper, to taste

For garnish
Fresh basil
Parmigiano-Reggiano or Parmesan, grated

Directions
1. Melt the butter in a deep frying pan or heavy-bottomed pot over medium-high heat.
2. Sauté the shallots until tender (about 2 minutes).
3. Add the cream and bring to a low boil.
4. Reduce the heat to medium low and simmer for 3 minutes.
5. Remove the pan from the heat and stir in the cheese, salt and pepper until smooth.
6. Add the cooked pasta and reserved pasta water to the sauce.
7. Return the pan to the stove over medium-high heat, and gently stir the pasta in the sauce to coat.
8. Garnish with Parmigiano-Reggiano and fresh basil, and serve.

Classic Lasagna

Serves: 10
Preparation Time: 1 hour 35 minutes
Cooking Time: 30 minutes

Ingredients
16 flat "no boil" lasagna noodles
4 cups mozzarella cheese, grated, divided

For meat sauce
1 large yellow onion, chopped
1 tablespoon olive oil
2 cloves garlic, peeled and minced
1 pound ground beef, preferably sirloin
1 pound ground Italian sausage
1 teaspoon kosher salt
1 tablespoon dried basil
1 tablespoon dried oregano
1 tablespoon dried parsley
12 ounces tomato paste

1 (28 ounce) can whole San Marzano tomatoes
¼ cup red wine or water

For cheese sauce
3 cups whole milk ricotta
2 eggs
2 tablespoons fresh parsley, chopped
½ teaspoon freshly ground black pepper
½ cup Parmesan cheese, freshly grated

Directions
For the meat sauce
1. Sauté the onion in olive oil over medium heat in a medium-sized pot.
2. Add the garlic, beef, and sausage and cook, with stirring, until browned.
3. Stir in the salt, basil, parsley, and oregano.
4. Stir in the tomato paste.
5. Scoop out the San Marzano tomatoes one by one, crushing each with your hand over the sauce to catch the juice. Drop the crushed tomato into the sauce as well.
6. Swirl the wine or water in the can to get remaining tomato juice and pour it into the pot. Stir, and reduce the heat to low.
7. Cover and let simmer for 45 minutes.

For the cheese sauce
8. In a large bowl, mix ricotta, eggs, parsley, black pepper, and Parmesan together.
9. Keep refrigerated until ready to assemble lasagna.

To assemble the lasagna

10. Preheat the oven to 375°F and grease a 13x9 baking pan.
11. Spread 1 cup of meat sauce on the bottom of the baking pan.
12. Arrange 4 lasagna noodles in a layer over the meat sauce.
13. Spread ⅓ of the cheese sauce on top, and sprinkle with about ½ cup of mozzarella
14. Continue layering, ending with meat sauce sprinkled with mozzarella.
15. Bake the lasagna until the cheese is golden (about 30-40 minutes).
16. Let sit for 10 minutes before serving.

Pasta with Vegetables (Primavera)

Serves: 6
Preparation Time: 25 minutes
Cooking Time: 20 minutes

Ingredients
3 carrots, peeled and julienned
2 medium zucchini or 1 large zucchini, julienned
2 yellow squash, julienned
1 onion, thinly sliced
1 yellow bell pepper, julienned
1 red bell pepper, julienned
¼ cup olive oil
Kosher salt and freshly ground black pepper
1 tablespoon dried Italian herbs
1 pound farfalle (bowtie pasta), cooked according to packaging instructions
15 cherry tomatoes, halved
½ cup grated Parmesan

Directions
1. Preheat the oven to 450°F.
2. Toss all the vegetables with the oil, salt, pepper, and dried herbs to coat.
3. Arrange the vegetables on 2 baking sheets, in a single layer. Do not crowd.
4. Bake until the vegetables begin to brown (about 20 minutes), stirring and flipping halfway through.
5. Drain the trays, and set aside about 1 cup of the liquid from the vegetables.
6. Combine the pasta, baked vegetables, cherry tomatoes, and reserved liquid.
7. Season with salt and pepper.
8. Sprinkle with the Parmesan and serve.

Creamy Pesto Linguini

Serves: 6
Preparation Time: 10 minutes
Cooking Time: 3 minutes

Ingredients
⅓ cup extra-virgin olive oil
½ cup heavy cream
2 tablespoons butter
1 (12 ounce) pack linguine pasta, cooked according to packaging instructions and drained

Pesto Sauce
¾ cup fresh basil leaves
¾ cup grated Parmesan cheese, divided
3 tablespoons pine nuts
2 cloves garlic, peeled
½ teaspoon kosher salt
½ teaspoon freshly ground pepper

Directions
1. To make the pesto, combine the basil, ½ cup of Parmesan cheese, pine nuts, garlic, salt, and pepper in a food processor. Pulse to combine.
2. Add the oil gradually, in drizzles, while processing.
3. In a saucepan, combine the butter and cream over medium heat.
4. Add the pesto to the cream mixture and stir, simmering for 3 minutes.
5. Remove from the heat, add the remaining Parmesan, and stir well.
6. Lastly, add the drained linguine and mix well.

Fettuccini Carbonara

Serves: 6
Preparation Time: 10 minutes
Cooking Time: 25 minutes

Ingredients
1 tablespoon olive oil
4 shallots, peeled and diced
1 large onion, peeled and sliced
1 pound bacon, cut into strips
1 clove garlic, chopped
1 (16 ounce) packet fettuccine, cooked according to packaging instructions
3 egg yolks
½ cup cream
¾ cup Parmesan cheese, shredded
Salt and pepper to taste

Directions

1. Drain the fettucine and place it in a serving dish or bowl. Set it aside.
2. In a large saucepan, heat the olive oil and sauté the shallots over medium heat until the shallots are softened.
3. Add the onion and bacon.
4. When bacon is just beginning to brown, stir in the garlic and remove the pot from the heat.
5. Meanwhile, whisk the eggs, cream, and Parmesan together in a bowl.
6. Pour the bacon mixture over pasta.
7. Add the cream mixture, salt, and pepper, and stir.

Seafood Linguini (Linguini al Fruiti di Mare)

Serves: 4
Preparation Time: 15 minutes
Cooking Time: 15 minutes

Ingredients
2 ¼ pounds mixed shellfish (like clams, mussels, scampi, unpeeled shrimp or prawns), cleaned
¼ cup dry white wine
25-30 cherry tomatoes, halved, seeded, and juiced
1 (16 ounce) pack dried linguine, cooked according to packaging directions, drained
½ cup olive oil
5 garlic cloves, thinly sliced
⅛ teaspoon dried chili flakes, or to taste
3 tablespoons flat leaf parsley, chopped
Salt and freshly ground black pepper, to taste

Directions

1. Start with the clams and mussels. After cleaning, put them in a pot with the wine.
2. Cover and cook over high heat until the shells have opened (about 4 minutes). Remove unopened shellfish and dispose. Set aside the opened clams and shellfish. Reserve all but about 2 tablespoons of the cooking liquid.
3. Chop the seeded, squeezed cherry tomatoes.
4. Meanwhile, put the olive oil and garlic into a large pan, and heat gently until the garlic begins to sizzle.
5. Add the chili flakes and chopped tomatoes, and simmer for 5 minutes.
6. Add the strained, reserved liquid from the clams and bring it again to a boil.
7. Simmer until the liquid is reduced.
8. Add the scampi into the sauce and cook until pink in color, flipping over once.
9. Add the prawns and simmer until cooked (about 3 minutes).
10. Stir in the cooked clams and mussels.
11. Add the parsley and continue cooking, turning over seafood occasionally, until heated through.
12. Season with a little salt and pepper, as desired.
13. Pour over cooked pasta and toss.

Shrimp in Spicy Sauce (Fra Diavolo)

Serves: 4
Preparation Time: 15 minutes
Cooking Time: 18 minutes

Ingredients
1 pound large shrimp, peeled and deveined
1 teaspoon salt, or as needed
1 teaspoon dried crushed red pepper flakes
4-5 tablespoons olive oil, divided
1 medium onion, sliced
1 (14 ½ ounce) can diced tomatoes, juice retained
1 cup dry white wine
3 cloves garlic, chopped
¼ teaspoon dried oregano leaves
3 tablespoon fresh Italian parsley leaves, chopped
3 tablespoon fresh basil leaves, chopped
Cooked pasta for serving

Directions

1. In a bowl, mix together the shrimp, salt, and red pepper flakes.
2. Heat 3 tablespoons of oil in a large skillet over medium-high heat.
3. Add shrimp and sauté until just cooked through (about 2 minutes). Place it in a dish and set it aside.
4. Using the same skillet, sauté the onion in 1 to 2 teaspoons of olive oil until translucent (about 5 minutes).
5. Add the undrained tomatoes, wine, garlic, and oregano.
6. Simmer until the sauce begins to thicken (about 10 minutes)
7. Return the shrimp and its juices to the tomato mixture.
8. Toss and cook about 1 minute longer.
9. Stir in the parsley, basil, and more salt as needed. Serve over pasta.

Pasta with Capers, Olives and Tomato (Puttanesca)

Serves: 4
Preparation Time: 10 minutes
Cooking Time: 25 minutes

Ingredients
1 (14 ounce) package spaghetti, cooked according to packaging instructions, drained
2 tablespoons olive oil
2 cloves garlic, chopped
1 small red chili, finely chopped
1 cup pitted black olives, sliced
6 sundried tomatoes, cut into thin strips
2 anchovy fillets, chopped (optional)
2 tablespoons salted capers, rinsed
1 (14 ½ ounce) can diced tomatoes
½ cup fresh basil leaves, shredded
Grated Parmesan, to serve

Directions

1. Heat the olive oil in a skillet over medium heat, and sauté the garlic and chili for 1 minute.
2. Add the olives, sundried tomatoes, capers, anchovies, and diced tomatoes, and simmer for 20 minutes. Season with pepper.
3. Add the pasta to the sauce, and season with basil.
4. Mix well.
5. Serve sprinkled with Parmesan.

Pizza

Basic Pizza Dough

Serves: 2 crusts, medium to large in size
Preparation Time: 2 hours 10 minutes
Cooking Time: 6-8 minutes (pre-baking)

Ingredients
1 tablespoon sugar
1 ⅓ cups warm water (105°F)
1 (¼ ounce) packet active dry yeast (2 ¼ teaspoons)
3 tablespoons extra-virgin olive oil, plus more for brushing
3 ¾ cups all-purpose flour, plus more for dusting
1 ½ teaspoons salt

Directions
1. Dissolve the sugar in warm water, and add the yeast. Let it sit until the water becomes frothy (about 10 minutes). Stir in the olive oil.
2. In a large bowl, mix the flour and salt together.
3. Make a well in the center and pour in the yeast mixture.
4. Using a wooden spoon, mix until a rough dough is formed.
5. Place the dough on a floured surface and knead until it becomes smooth and elastic (about 5 minutes).
6. Prepare two bowls and brush them with olive oil.
7. Divide the dough in half as equally as possible (about 1 pound per piece).
8. Place each portion of dough in a prepared bowl, and brush the surface with oil.
9. Cover with plastic wrap and allow the dough to expand to double its size (about 1 hour and 30 minutes).
10. Roll out into desired shape and diameter. The dough may be covered with plastic wrap and stored, frozen, for 1 month.
11. If pre-baked crust is required, bake at 425°F until lightly browned (about 6-8 minutes).

Homemade Pizza Sauce

Serves: 2-4
Preparation Time: 15 minutes
Cooking Time: 1 hours 10 minutes

Ingredients
1 (28 ounce) can whole peeled tomatoes
1 tablespoon extra-virgin olive oil
1 tablespoon unsalted butter
2 medium cloves garlic, grated
2 anchovy fillets (optional)
1 teaspoon dried oregano
Pinch red pepper flakes
⅛ teaspoon kosher salt, or to taste
2 sprigs fresh basil, leaves attached
1 medium yellow onion, peeled and halved
1 teaspoon sugar
⅛ cup red wine (optional)

Directions
1. Make the tomatoes into a chunky (not smooth) consistency using a blender, food processor or food mill. Set aside.
2. Heat the oil and butter over low to medium heat in a saucepan.
3. When the butter has melted, add the garlic, anchovy (optional), oregano, pepper flakes, and salt. If using anchovies, mash them with a wooden spoon or with a fork as you sauté.
4. Stir while cooking until the garlic has browned slightly (about 3-4 minutes).
5. Add the chopped tomatoes, basil, onion, sugar, and red wine (optional).
6. Simmer, stirring occasionally, over very low heat until reduced by ½ (about 1 hour).
7. Remove the onion and basil stems.
8. Adjust the flavor with salt or more pepper flakes, according to taste.
9. Allow to cool to room temperature.
10. Will keep in the refrigerator for 2 weeks.

Cheese Pizza

Serves: 8
Preparation Time: 5 minutes plus 45 minutes freezing time
Cooking Time: 10-12 minutes

Ingredients
1 (12 inch) round of pizza dough
¼ -⅓ cup pizza sauce or all-purpose tomato sauce
2 cups mozzarella cheese, shredded and then frozen
1 tablespoon fresh basil, chopped finely

Directions
1. Preheat the oven to 450°F 45 minutes to an hour before baking.
2. Keep the grated mozzarella in the freezer for at least 20 minutes.
3. Place the pizza dough on a greased baking pan or pizza stone.

4. Spread the sauce from center of the dough outward, leaving about half an inch of space around the edge.
5. Sprinkle uniformly with shredded mozzarella and basil.
6. Bake until the crust is set and the cheese bubbles (about 10-12 minutes).
7. Best served hot.

Hawaiian Pizza

Serves: 8-12
Preparation Time: 10 minutes
Cooking Time: 21 minutes

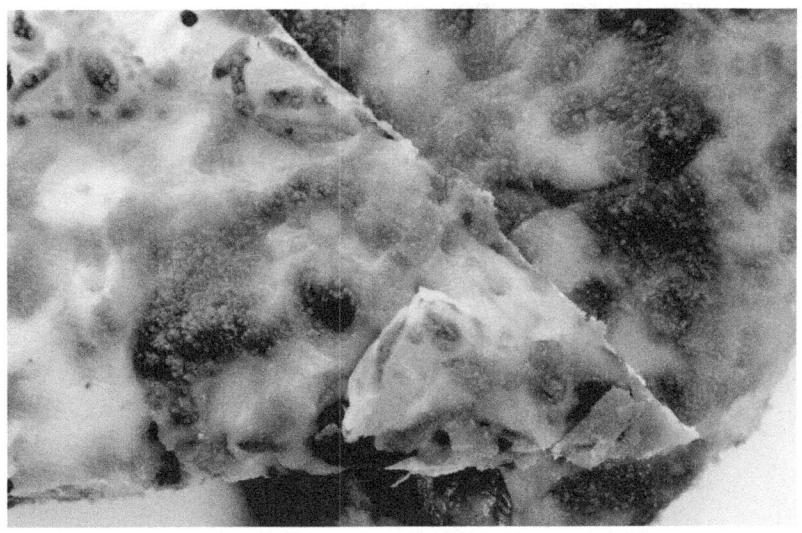

Ingredients
1 (15 inch) round of pizza dough
1 ¾ cups pizza sauce
2 cups shredded mozzarella cheese, divided
1 cup shredded Romano cheese, divided
1 ½ cup cooked ham, diced
1 cup pineapple tidbits, drained

Directions
1. Preheat the oven to 425°F and grease a 15-inch pizza pan.
2. Press the dough into pan, building up the edges slightly.
3. Bake until lightly browned (about 6-8 minutes).

4. Spread the sauce, beginning from the center of the crust going outward in a circular motion, leaving half an inch of space around the edge.
5. Sprinkle with 1 ¾ cups of mozzarella and ½ cup of Romano cheese.
6. Arrange ham and pineapple on top, and sprinkle with the remaining cheese.
7. Bake until the cheese is melted and crust is golden brown (about 15 minutes).

Super Meat Pizza

Serves: 8
Preparation Time: 25 minutes
Cooking Time: 15 minutes

Ingredients
Pizza dough, rolled out to make 15-inch crust or 15- by 10-inch rectangular crust
½ pound lean ground beef
½ pound Italian sausage, casing removed
½ cup pizza sauce
½ cup sliced pepperoni
1 ounce thinly sliced salami, cut into quarters
½ cup prosciutto or bacon, diced
1 cup cheddar cheese, shredded
1 cup mozzarella cheese, shredded

Directions
1. Preheat the oven to 400°F.
2. Grease the pan for the pizza dough. Press the dough to fit the pan.
3. Using a nonstick frying pan, cook the beef and sausage over medium-high heat, with constant stirring. The beef should be well done and the sausage no longer pink (about 6 to 8 minutes). Remove from the pan and drain on paper towels.
4. Spread the pizza sauce to within half an inch of the edges of the dough.
5. Add the drained beef and sausage.
6. Arrange all the other ingredients over the pizza.
7. Bake until the crust is golden brown and the cheese is melted (13 to 16 minutes).

Pepperoni Pizza

Serves: 8
Preparation Time: 2 hours 20 minutes
Cooking Time: 15 minutes

Ingredients
Pizza dough, rolled into a 13-inch diameter crust
1 tablespoon olive oil
½ cup pizza sauce
2 cups mozzarella cheese, grated
¼ cup Parmesan cheese, finely grated
30 slices Italian pepperoni
⅛ teaspoon crushed red pepper flakes
Fresh basil leaves for grnish

Directions

1. Preheat the oven to 450°F.
2. Place pizza dough on a greased pan.
3. Brush olive oil over the entire top of the pizza dough.
4. Spread pizza sauce over the dough, leaving about half an inch of dough around the edges for the crust.
5. Spread Parmesan evenly over sauce, the followed by mozzarella.
6. Arrange the Italian pepperoni on top.
7. Bake until the crust is golden brown and the cheese is melted (about 12-15 minutes).
8. Let cool for about 10 minutes, and sprinkle with basil leaves.

Pesto Veggie Pizza

Serves: 6
Preparation Time: 25 minutes
Cooking Time: 10 minutes

Ingredients
1 prebaked 12-inch thin pizza crust dough
2 cups fresh mushrooms, sliced
1 cup fresh broccoli florets, chopped
¾ cup zucchini, thinly sliced
½ cup sweet yellow pepper, julienned
½ cup sweet red pepper, julienned
1 small red onion, thinly sliced and separated into rings
1 tablespoon pesto sauce
½ cup pizza sauce or all-purpose tomato sauce
¼ cup grated Romano or Parmesan cheese
¼ cup ripe olives, sliced
¾ cup shredded mozzarella cheese

Directions
1. Preheat the oven to 450°F.
2. Place a pre-baked crust in a pizza pan or on a pizza stone.
3. Meanwhile, coat a skillet with non-stick cooking spray or vegetable oil and heat over medium heat.
4. Sauté the mushrooms, broccoli, zucchini, peppers, and onion until tender.
5. Remove from the heat and stir in the pesto. Set the pan aside.
6. Spread the pizza sauce over the pizza crust.
7. Arrange the sautéed vegetables and olives, and sprinkle with the cheeses
8. Bake until the crust is golden brown and the cheese has melted (about 10-12 minutes).

Italian Spicy Sausage and Mushrooms Pizza

Serves: 6
Preparation Time: 10 minutes plus 15 minutes resting time for dough
Cooking Time: 25-30 minutes

Ingredients
1 pound refrigerated ready-made or homemade pizza dough
Cooking spray
6 ounces spicy talian sausage (1 large sausage)
1 cup onion, thinly sliced
1 (8 ounce) package mushrooms, sliced
1 cup red or green bell pepper, seeded and diced
1 tablespoon yellow cornmeal, or more, for dusting
½ cup pizza sauce or all-purpose tomato sauce
½ cup shredded mozzarella cheese
¼ cup grated Parmigiano-Reggiano cheese

Directions
1. Rest the refrigerated dough for 15 minutes.
2. Preheat the oven to 450°F.
3. Remove the sausage from the casing and cook it in a nonstick skillet until it crumbles (about 3 minutes). Break it up with your spatula as it cooks.
4. Add the onions and mushrooms and sauté until tender (about 4 minutes).
5. Add the bell pepper and sauté until fragrant (about 3 minutes).
6. Dust work surface with cornmeal.
7. Pat and stretch the dough gently and place it on the dusted surface.
8. Press it down and spread it with your hands, and then roll it out with a dusted rolling pin to make a 12-inch round.
9. Place the dough on the pizza pan, stretching and shaping it with your hands if needed.
10. Pour the pizza sauce in the center of the dough and spread it to the sides, leaving about half an inch from edge without sauce.
11. Spread with the sausage and vegetable mixture.
12. Top with mozzarella and then with Parmesan.
13. Bake until the cheese is golden brown and bubbly (about 15-20 minutes).

White Pizza (Pizza Bianca) with Chicken and Broccoli

Serves: 15
Preparation Time: 15 minutes
Cooking Time: 20 minutes

Ingredients
1 recipe pizza dough
1 tablespoon dried parsley flakes
1 tablespoon dried chopped onion
2 skinless chicken breasts, pre-grilled or sautéed, cubed
1 (13 ounce) pack frozen broccoli florets, thawed
4 cups shredded mozzarella cheese, divided
3 tablespoons Parmesan cheese, or as desired

Directions
1. Preheat the oven to 450°F.
2. Pat and stretch the pizza dough to fit a lightly greased cookie sheet.
3. Sprinkle the dough with chopped onion and parsley flakes.
4. Bake, on the lower rack, for 5 minutes.
5. Remove the pan from the oven and let it cool for about 10 minutes, then sprinkle with 3 cups of mozzarella.
6. Add broccoli and chicken.
7. Meanwhile, reduce the oven temperature to 350°F.
8. Top the pizza with the remaining mozzarella cheese.
9. Place the pizza on the middle rack, and bake to heat ingredients and melt the cheese (about 15 minutes).
10. Sprinkle with Parmesan, cut, and serve.

BBQ Chicken Pizza

Serves: 6-8
Preparation Time: 5 minutes
Cooking Time: 8-12 minutes

Ingredients
1 (12 inch) pre-baked pizza crust
¼ cup pizza sauce
¼ cup barbecue sauce
1 cup cooked chicken, shredded
2 cups Italian 5 cheese blend, shredded
8 garlic cloves, roasted
1 red onion, sliced
Italian parsley, for garnish

Directions
1. Preheat the oven to 450°F.
2. Place the pre-baked crust on a pizza pan or pizza stone.
3. Mix the pizza and barbecue sauce together, then spread it on the crust.
4. Spread with 1 cup cheese.
5. Add the chicken, garlic, and onion.
6. Top with the remaining cheese.
7. Bake the pizza until the cheese is melted and bubbling (about 8-12 minutes). Sprinkle with parsley.
8. Cut and serve.

Chicken

Chicken Marsala

Serves: 4
Preparation Time: 20 minutes
Cooking Time: 20 minutes

Ingredients
4 boneless skinless chicken breast halves, pounded thin
Salt, to taste
Freshly ground pepper, to taste
½ teaspoon dried oregano
Pinch each of marjoram and thyme (optional)
2 tablespoons olive oil
2 tablespoons butter
½ cup pancetta or bacon, chopped
2 shallots, finely chopped
½ pound mushrooms, sliced
½ teaspoon garlic powder
½ cup dry Marsala

1 ½ cups heavy cream
1 teaspoon lemon juice
Fresh parsley, chopped, for garnish

Directions
1. Pound the chicken breasts to an even thickness.
2. Season with salt, pepper, and oregano (marjoram and thyme also, if desired).
3. Heat the oil in a skillet over medium-high heat, and sear the chicken until golden brown (about 2 minutes on each side). Transfer to a plate and set aside.
4. Melt the remaining butter in the pan and add the pancetta, shallots, mushrooms, and garlic powder.
5. Cook until the mushrooms and shallots are lightly browned.
6. Add the Marsala and bring it to a boil, scraping any browned bits from the bottom of the pan.
7. Add the cream and lemon juice, and return it to a boil.
8. Simmer until the sauce is reduced and begins to thicken.
9. Return the chicken to pan to heat through (about 3 minutes).
10. Serve garnished with parsley.

Chicken Parmigiana

Serves: 4
Preparation Time: 30 minutes
Cooking Time: 45 minutes

Ingredients
4 pieces boneless skinless chicken breast, pounded thin
Salt and pepper
1 large egg, beaten with ½ tablespoon water
½ cup all-purpose flour
1 cup panko bread crumbs
¼ cup vegetable oil
All-Purpose Tomato Sauce, recipe below
1 pound fresh mozzarella, thinly sliced
¼ cup freshly grated Parmesan
Sliced green onion, for garnish
Fettuccini with tomato sauce for serving

All-Purpose Tomato Sauce

2 tablespoons olive oil
1 large onion, finely chopped
4 cloves garlic, smashed to a paste with a pinch of salt
2 (28 ounce) cans plum tomatoes, undrained, pureed in a blender
1 (16 ounce) can crushed tomatoes
1 (2 ½ ounce) can tomato paste
1 bay leaf
½ cup Italian parsley
1 small yellow bell pepper, chopped
Salt and freshly ground pepper

Directions

For the sauce
1. In a saucepan, heat the olive oil over medium heat.
2. Cook the onions and garlic until they are soft.
3. Add the pureed tomatoes with their juices, crushed tomatoes, tomato paste, bay leaf, parsley, and bell pepper, and bring it to a boil. Season to taste with salt and pepper.
4. Reduce the heat and cook until slightly thickened, about 30 minutes.
5. Let cool to room temperature and store, refrigerated, in jars.

For the chicken
6. Preheat the oven to 400°F.
7. Season the chicken with salt and pepper
8. Coat with flour and tap lightly to remove any excess.
9. Dip in the egg mixture and all any excess to drip off.
10. Coat evenly with bread crumbs.

11. In a skillet on the stovetop, heat the oil almost to the smoking point.
12. Brown the breasts on both sides (about 30-40 seconds per side).
13. Transfer the chicken to a baking sheet.
14. Top each chicken piece with 1-2 tablespoons of tomato sauce, slices of mozzarella and about 1 tablespoon of Parmesan.
15. Season with salt and pepper.
16. Bake until the chicken is cooked through and the cheese is melted (about 5 to 7 minutes).
17. Garnish with green onion and serve over pasta with tomato sauce if desired.

Dessert (Dolci)

Tiramisu

Serves: 2
Preparation Time: 15 minutes plus 2 hours refrigeration
Cooking Time: 0 minutes

Ingredients
4 pieces ladyfinger biscuit
¼ teaspoon cocoa powder for dusting

Mascarpone Mixture
1 egg yolk, should be very fresh, preferably free-range
2 tablespoons sugar
1 teaspoon vanilla essence
1 cup mascarpone
2 teaspoons milk, or as needed

Espresso Dip
1 cup espresso, warm
1 tablespoon Kahlua (optional)
1 tablespoon sugar

Directions
Mascarpone Mixture
1. Whisk the yolk, sugar, and vanilla essence until well blended, then mix in the mascarpone.
2. Add the milk gradually to soften the mixture if the mascarpone is too stiff.
3. Whisk until blended.

Espresso Dip
4. Mix the ingredients together until the sugar is dissolved completely.

To assemble the Tiramisu
5. Prepare 2 dessert bowls or cups.
6. Soak a ladyfinger in espresso and break it in half. Place it in the bowl/cup as the first layer.
7. Follow with about ¼ of the mascarpone mixture.
8. Soak and break another lady finger for the third layer.
9. Top with another layer of mascarpone and dust by passing cocoa powder through a sieve over the dessert cup.
10. Repeat for second dessert bowl.
11. Refrigerate for 2 hours and serve.

Homemade Cannoli

Serves: 12-25
Preparation Time: 20 minutes plus 2 hours refrigeration
Cooking Time: 10-15 minutes

Ingredients
Egg white, for sealing
Oil for frying, 3 inches deep

Cannoli shell
2 ⅓ cups flour
1 ½ tablespoons sugar
2 tablespoons butter
1 egg
⅛ teaspoon salt
¾ cup Marsala dry wine

Cream Filling
2 cups ricotta cheese
2 cups confectioner's sugar, sifted

2 tablespoons rum
¼ teaspoon vanilla extract
3 ounces bitter chocolate, broken into tiny chips

Directions
To make the shells
1. In a large bowl, mix the shell ingredients together to make a smooth, slightly sticky dough.
2. Wrap the dough in plastic wrap and refrigerate for 2 hours to overnight.
3. Cut the dough into two pieces. Keep the remaining dough covered and cold while you work.
4. Lightly flour a work surface and roll out the dough to about ⅛ inch thick.
5. Cut out circles, 3 to 5 inches in diameter.
6. Roll each cut out circle into an oval.
7. Oil the outside of the cannoli tubes. You can also use cannelloni pasta as tubes.
8. Roll the ovals around each tube and dab a little egg white on the dough where the edges overlap. Press well to seal. Let them sit for the egg white to set.
9. In a heavy saucepan or electric deep-fryer, heat the oil to 375°F, or until a small piece of the dough sizzles and browns in 1 minute.
10. Fry the shells until golden, turning halfway through (about 2 minutes).
11. Lift with a wire skimmer or large slotted spoon. Using tongs, grasp the cannoli vertically over the fryer to let the oil flow back into the pan.
12. Drain on paper towels. Repeat with the remaining tubes.

13. While still hot, grasp the tubes with a potholder and, using a pair of tongs, pull the cannoli shells off.
14. Let cool completely on the paper towels.

For the filling
15. In a large bowl, cream the ricotta with a wire whisk.
16. Add the rest of the ingredients and mix thoroughly.
17. Fill a pastry tube, and pipe the filling into the shells.
18. Dust with confectioner's sugar, and serve.

Conclusion

Italian-American cuisine is so imbedded in American food culture that it may now be considered truly American. It is no wonder that America has fully embraced Italian-inspired dishes. Though modified through the years as Italian immigrants assimilated into American culture, the spirit and passion of authentic Italian cooking still remains. Italian food will always be comfort food and this cookbook gives us all the opportunity to bring this comfort into our homes.

Buon appetito!

Image Credits

Pasta and Beans Soup (Pasta e Fagioli)

Chris "Mojo" Denbow from Houston, USA (Pasta e Fagioli) [CC BY 2.0 (http://creativecommons.org/licenses/by/2.0)], via Wikimedia Commons

Also from Lina Chang

Appendix
Cooking Conversion Charts

1. Volumes

US Fluid Oz.	US	US Dry Oz.	Metric Liquid ml
¼ oz.	2 tsp.	1 oz.	10 ml.
½ oz.	1 tbsp.	2 oz.	15 ml.
1 oz.	2 tbsp.	3 oz.	30 ml.
2 oz.	¼ cup	3½ oz.	60 ml.
4 oz.	½ cup	4 oz.	125 ml.
6 oz.	¾ cup	6 oz.	175 ml.
8 oz.	1 cup	8 oz.	250 ml.

Tsp.= teaspoon - tbsp.= tablespoon – oz.= ounce – ml.= millimeter

2. Oven Temperatures

Celsius (°C)	Fahrenheit (°F)
90	220
110	225
120	250
140	275
150	300
160	325
180	350
190	375
200	400
215	425
230	450
250	475
260	500

Made in United States
Orlando, FL
23 December 2024